Jacob's Dream!

**A Story on People and Cultures
from different Countries
Ronald W. Holmes, Ph.D.**

AuthorHouse™
1663 Liberty Drive
Bloomington, IN 47403
www.authorhouse.com
Phone: 833-262-8899

This book is printed on acid-free paper.

ISBN: 978-1-7283-6812-2 (sc)
ISBN: 978-1-7283-6813-9 (e)

Library of Congress Control Number: 2020913512

Print information available on the last page.

Published by AuthorHouse 07/24/2020

author HOUSE®

Jacob's Dream!

A Story on People and Cultures from different Countries

Introduction

Jacob is a boy who is very curious about things and often has a lot of dreams. He has dreamt about the solar system, flowers, colors, careers, continents, animals, birds, and bullying. In this book, Jacob dreams about various people and cultures from different countries. He is particularly curious about why some people are dark and light complexion (like himself).

Jacob learns that dark-skinned people have more melanin in their skin than light-skinned people have in their skin. Melanin is a natural skin pigment that plays a role in the color of human's skin, hair, and eyes.

CHINA

KIM

While sleeping, Jacob is in a dream. He visits China, India, Nigeria, Ethiopia, Mexico, and England before returning back to the United States. During his visits to these countries, Jacob meets several people who introduce him to the culture in their countries. The first person Jacob meets in China is Kim Ming.

Coloring Your Own

CHINA

KIM

In Jacob's dream, Jacob meets Kim Ming.

Welcome to China Jacob! China is the world's largest populated country. Chinese people have melanin in their skin. It causes our skin to have some color. There are seven different forms of the Chinese language spoken. Mandarin Chinese is the most common language, and is the oldest written language in the world. About 850 million people speak Mandarin.

Coloring Your Own

CHINA

KIM

Also Jacob,

Bejing is one of our four major cities in China and is also known as one of the capital cities. The other three capitals are Nanjing, Luoyang, and Chang'an. Tiananmen Square is the largest city square in the world; it is in Bejing. Ping Pong is the most popular sport in China, and on the average there are about 300 million people who play it. Some of our favorite foods are rice, bean sprouts, cabbage, scallions, and tofu. Each year we celebrate the Lunar New Year between the middle of January and February. This a special time to celebrate our ancestors.

India

Annika

The second country Jacob visits and learns about is India.

Coloring Your Own

India

Annika

In Jacob's dream, Jacob meets Annika Sharon.

Welcome to India Jacob! India is one of the oldest cultures in the world. Indian people have melanin in their skin. It causes our skin to have color. Some people have more melanin than others, which makes some people darker than others. People started living in India 4,500 years ago. Approximately, 1.2 billion people live in India. India has 28 states and our most popular spoken language is Hindi. There are 22 other languages spoken in India.

Coloring Your Own

India

Annika

Also Jacob,

Our people write in a script called Devanagari. India is also known for its food, film, dance, and music. Wheat and basmati rice are staples in Indian dishes; in addition to, spices like curry, ginger, turmeric, and hot peppers. A large population of Indians are vegetarian but lamb and chicken are popular meat choices. Women in my country wear a colorful silk sari and the men wear something called a dhoti. The most important holiday we celebrate is called Diwali.

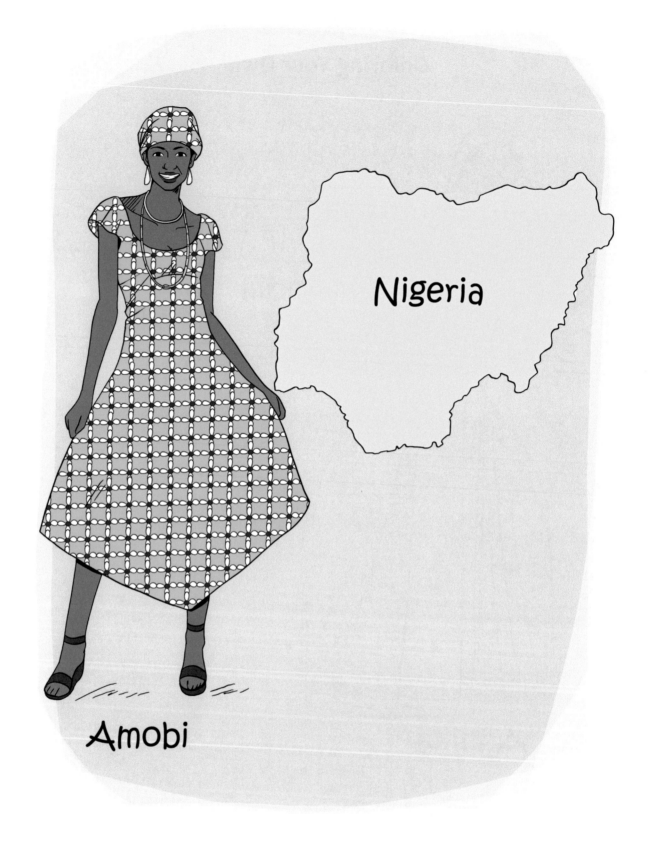

Nigeria

Amobi

The third country Jacob visits and learns about is Nigeria.

Coloring Your Own

Nigeria

Amobi

In Jacob's dream, Jacob meets Amobi Alibu.

Welcome to Nigeria Jacob! Nigeria is the largest Black nation in the world and is the largest country in Africa. Nigerian people have melanin in their skin. It causes our skin to have color. Some people have more melanin in their skin than others, which makes them darker than other people. Approximately, 180 million people live in Nigeria. Our capital cities are Abuja and Lagos. Lagos is the largest city in our country. We are the 8th most populated country in the world. Nigerians speak English but there are several different languages spoken by people.

Coloring Your Own

Amobi

Also Jacob,

The Yoruba people of Western Nigeria are known for their artwork and sculptures. The Igbos people of South Eastern Nigeria are known for their business sense. Our country's national sport is football (soccer). Nigeria has won the African cup of Nations several times. The most common foods we eat are rice, beans, yams, millet, cassava, and plantains. We are known for our trendy and highly fashionable clothing. Men and women like to wear colorful styles. Buba is a loose-fitting style of clothing that is most popular with both men and women. There are more men than women in Nigeria.

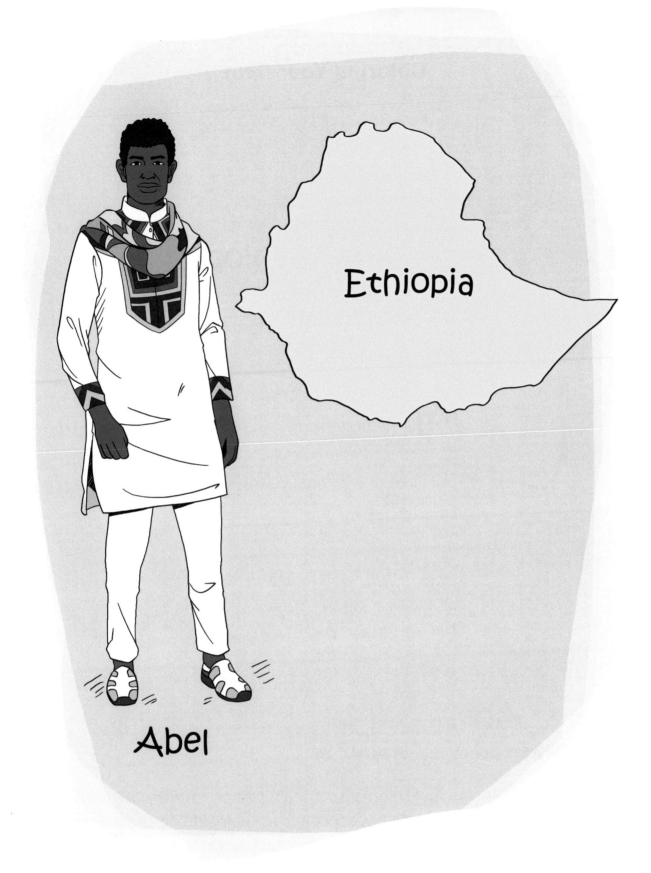

Ethiopia

Abel

The fourth country Jacob visits and learns about is Ethiopia.

Coloring Your Own

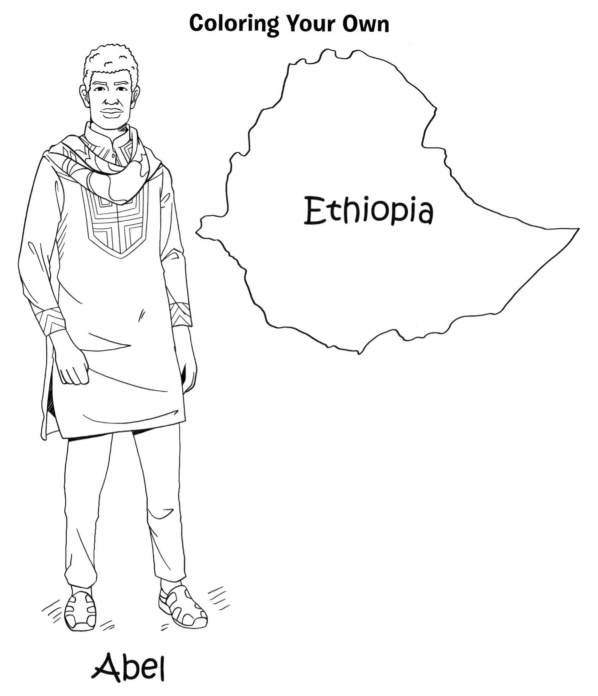

Ethiopia

Abel

In Jacob's dream, Jacob meets Abel.

Welcome to Ethiopia Jacob! Ethiopia is Africa's oldest country to gain its independence. Ethiopian people have melanin in their skin. It causes our skin to have color. Some Ethiopia people have more melanin in their skin, which makes them darker than others. Approximately 106 million people live in Ethiopia. Our capital city is Addis Abba which is the highest city in Africa. It sits above sea level. The Ethiopian wolf is one of the rarest animal, with only 500 remaining in the wild. Ethiopia is the only country with its time structure and has 13 months in a year. Ethiopia is seven years behind the traditional calendar.

Coloring Your Own

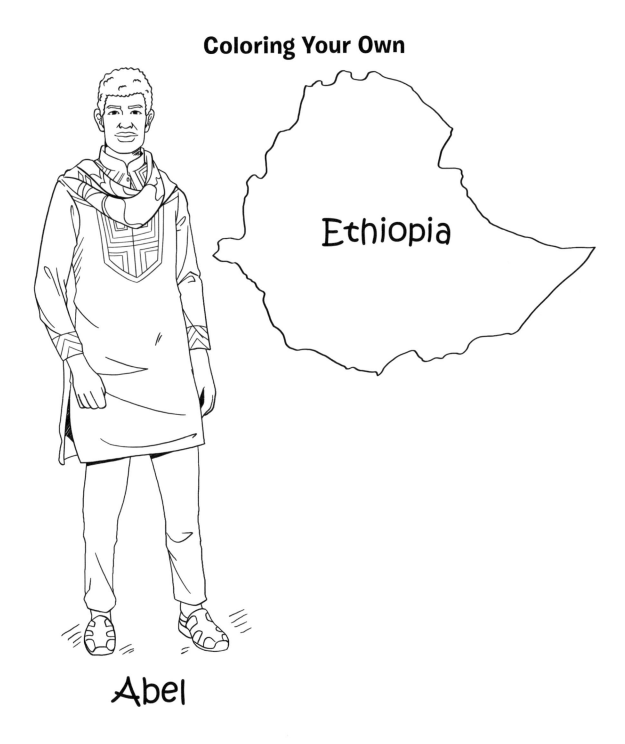

Ethiopia

Abel

Also Jacob,

There are 84 spoken languages in Ethiopia, but English is the main language that is widely spoken throughout the country and taught in schools and universities. Coffee is one of our most favorite drinks. We mostly eat vegetables and meats prepared as a stew. This is often served with a sourdough bread. Football is the most popular sport in Ethiopia.

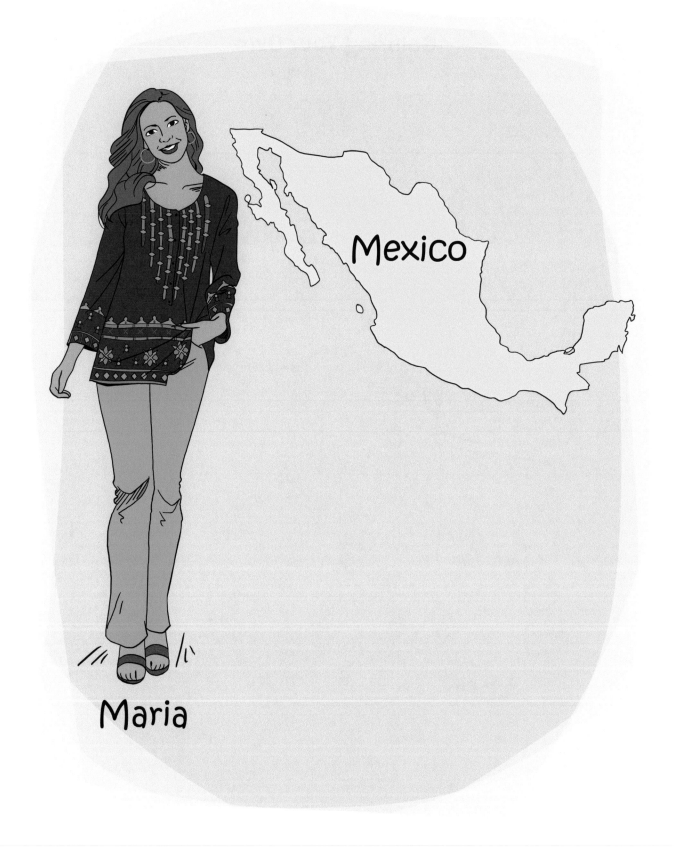

Mexico

Maria

The fifth country Jacob visits and learns about is Mexico.

Coloring Your Own

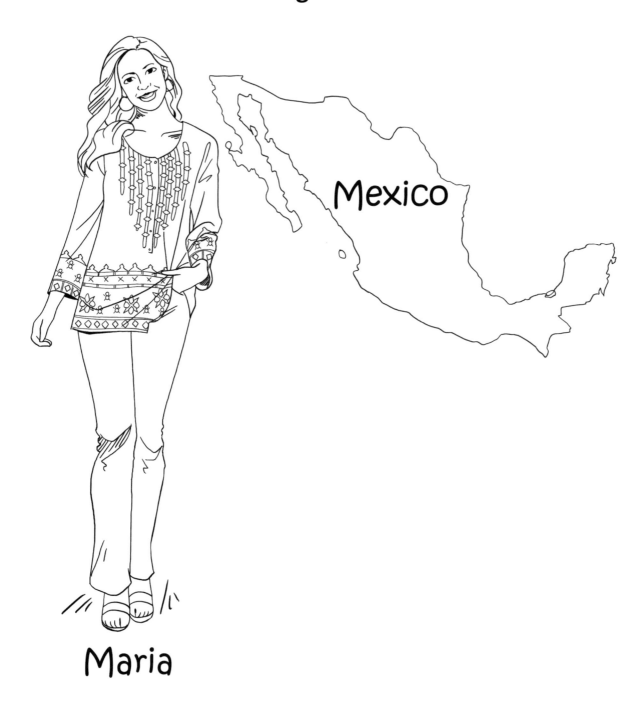

Mexico

Maria

In Jacob's dream, Jacob meets Maria Hernandez.

Welcome to Mexico Jacob! Mexico is the 12th largest populated country in the world. Mexican people have melanin in our skin. It causes our skin to have color. Some people have more melanin in their skin, which makes them darker than others. Approximately, 123 million people live in Mexico and Spanish is spoken by 92 percent of the people.

Coloring Your Own

Maria

Mexico

Also Jacob,

Some of our favorite foods in Mexico are tortillas, corn, peppers, and tomatoes. Women wear embroidered tops with patterns that have symbolic meanings and men wear large blanket shirts that are called sarape. In Mexico, we have a special day of celebration on December 12, The Feast of Our Lady Guadalupe.

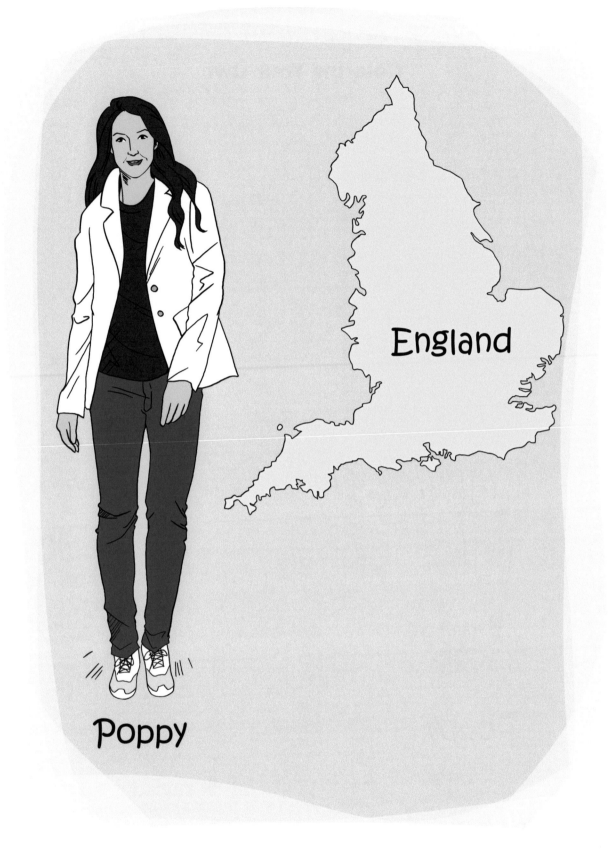

England

Poppy

The sixth country Jacob visits and learns about is England.

Coloring Your Own

England

Poppy

In Jacob's dream, Jacob meets Ms. Poppy.

Welcome to England Jacob! England is in the United Kingdom also known as the UK. English people are mostly Caucasian and have low levels of melanin in our skin. This causes us to be a blush white color. Approximately, 53 million people live in England, and English is spoken language by all people in England. The London Bridge is a famous attraction in London, England.

Coloring Your Own

England

Poppy

Also Jacob,

Some of our favorite foods in England are fish and chips, Eccles cake, black pudding, and Shepard's Pie. English people are fashionable. Some typical clothing includes jeans, t-shirts, tennis shoes, and tweed jackets. Some of the most popular music groups come from England such as The Beatles.

Reginald

Don

While sleeping, Jacob is in a dream. Jacob returns back home and learns about African Americans.

Coloring Your Own

Reginald Don

In Jacob's dream, Jacob meets Reginald Smith.

Welcome home Jacob! In the United States, there are all different types of people living in America such as Chinese, Indian, Nigerian, Ethiopian, Mexican, English, White Americans, and African Americans. African Americans, for example, have different shades of skin color. Some African Americans have more melanin in their skin, which causes them to be darker than other African Americans and White Americans.

Coloring Your Own

Reginald   Don

Also Jacob,

African Americans are the largest ethnic group in the United States. African Americans are connected to many different African cultures. Soul food is our most popular type of food. This includes fried chicken, macaroni and cheese, collard greens and fried okra. Some of the most popular music groups come from the United States. Jazz and the blues are popular among African Americans. Some of the most influential music is written and sung by African Americans.

Jacob's Dream!
A Lesson on People and Cultures from Different Countries

Teacher's Five Day
Lesson Plan

Grade	3
About the lesson	Jacob's dream, People and Cultures," introduces children to people from different backgrounds and cultures. In this lesson, students will read Jacob's Dream, discuss text-based guided questions, and key vocabulary. This will assist with helping student gain a deeper understanding of the text.
Highlighted Text	Jacob's Dream! A Lesson on People and Cultures from Different Countries
Standards Addressed- Key Ideas & Details	CCSS.ELA-LITERACY.RL.3.1 Ask and answer such questions as who, what, where, when, why, and how to demonstrate understanding of key details in a text. CCSS.ELA-LITERACY.RL.3.5 Describe the overall structure of a story, including how the beginning introduces the story and the ending concludes the action. CCSS.ELA-LITERACY.RI.3.5 Determine the meaning of words and phrases in a text relevant to a grade 2 topic or subject area.

Daily Plan

Day 1-Monday	1. Introduce Jacob's Dream to students 2. Facilitate a discussion of the background knowledge students have about the people and cultures represented in the book 3. Allow students to discuss any new information they've learned about people and cultures
Day 2- Tuesday	1. Handout copies of Jacob's Dream to each student 2. Guide students through a picture-walk and discuss text features 3. Facilitate a discussion about the text features, genre of book, and help students set a purpose for reading
Day 3- Wednesday	1. Read story aloud to students while they follow along 2. Pause and discuss after reading about each culture 3. Facilitate a discussion about the unique characteristics of each culture
Day 4- Thursday	1. Pair students with a buddy to re-read Jacob's Dream; assign each pair 1 or 2 cultures to read 2. Provide pre-written questions about the cultures for students to discuss with their buddy 3. Allow students time to share their responses with the class
Day 5- Friday	1. Instruct students to write characteristics about their cultures and families that make them unique and special
Reference	Holmes, Joi (2020). Developer, Lesson Plan

References

Holmes, R. (2020). Jacob's Dream! A Lesson on Flowers and Colors. Bloomington, IN: Authorhouse.

Holmes, R. (2019). Jacob's Dream! A Story on the Solar System. Bloomington, IN: Authorhouse.

Holmes, R. (2016). Jacob's Dream! A Lesson on Numbers and Birds. Bloomington, IN: Authorhouse.

Holmes, R. (2016). A Story of Bullying in School and Ways to Stop It. Bloomington, IN: AuthorHouse

Holmes, R. ((2015). Jacob's Dram! A Lesson on Alphabets and Continents. Bloomington, IN: AuthorHouse

Holmes, R. (2015). A Story of Animals in Africa. Bloomington, IN: AuthorHouse

Holmes, R. (2015). A Story of Careers for Children. Bloomington, IN: AuthorHouse

Live Science. Chinese Culture: Customs and traditions of China. Retrieved January 26, 2020 from, https://www.livescience.com/amp/28823-chinese-culture.html

Live Science. Indian Culture: Traditions and customs of India. Retrieved January 26, 2020 from, https://www.livescience.com/amp/28634-indian-culture.html

New World Excyclopedia. Culture of England. Retrieved January 26, 2020 from, https://www.newworldencyclopedia.org/entry/Culture_of_England

World Population Review. Largest countries in Africa 2020. Retrieved January 26, 2020 from, http://worldpopulationreview.com/countries/largest-countries-in-africa/

Printed in the United States
By Bookmasters